Published in the United States
by Xist Publishing
www.xistpublishing.com
24200 Southwest Freeway
Suite 402- 290
Rosenberg, TX 77471

Hardcover ISBN: 978-1-5324-3165-4
Paperback ISBN: 978-1-5324-3025-1
eISBN: 978-1-5324-3000-8

Printed in the USA

xist Publishing

OUT OF THIS WORLD

ILLUSTRATED SPACE JOKES FOR KIDS

Stephanie Rodriguez
Jenna Johnston

What was the first animal in space?

The cow that jumped over the moon.

What kind of stars wear sunglasses?

Movie stars.

Why is Saturn so rich?

Because it has lots of rings!

What kind of plates do they use in space?

Flying saucers!

Where do astronauts keep their sandwiches?

In a launch box!

Why is there no air in space?

Because the Milky Way would go bad.

How do the aliens get their baby to sleep?

They ROCKET!

Have you heard about the cow astronaut?

He landed on the mooooooon!

What did Earth say to the other planets?

You guys have no life.

Why did the sun go to school?

To get brighter!

Where do planets and stars go to study?

UNIVERSity!

What happened to the astronaut who stepped on chewing gum?

He got stuck in Orbit!

Why can't aliens play golf in space?

To many black holes.

What did the alien say to the cat?

Take me to your litter.

Knock knock.

Who's there?

Thermos.

Thermos who?

Thermos be a way to fly this thing!

What did Mars say to Saturn?

Give me a ring sometime!

Why wasn't the moon hungry?

Because it was full!

How do you throw a party for an astronaut?

You have to plan-et.

What does an astronaut use to keep his feet warm?

A space heater.

Knock knock.

Who's there?

Sunshine.

Sunshine who?

Sunshine on my shoulder makes me happy.

What do you give an alien?

Some space!

Check out the other Illustrated Joke Books from Xist Publishing:

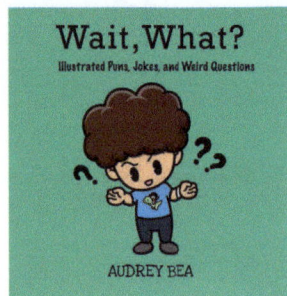

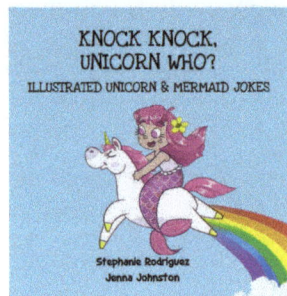

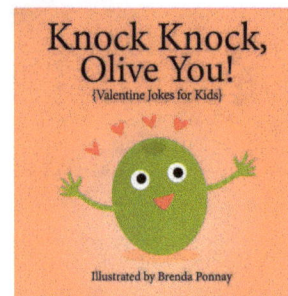

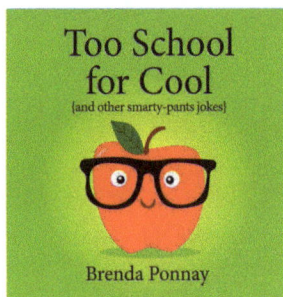

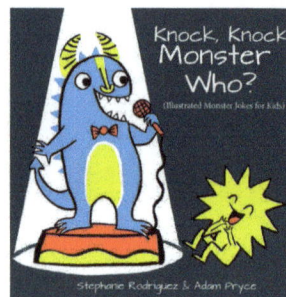

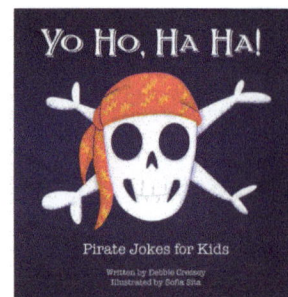

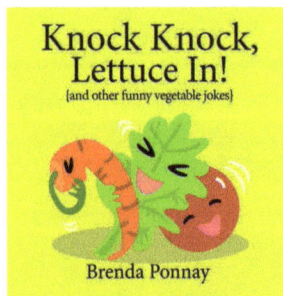

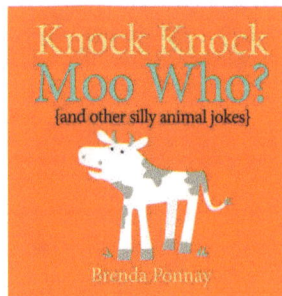

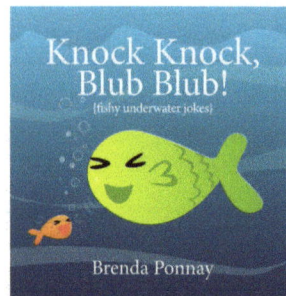

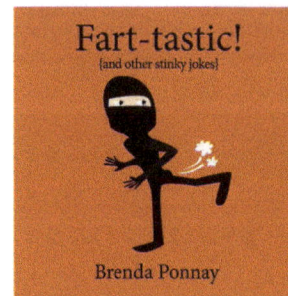

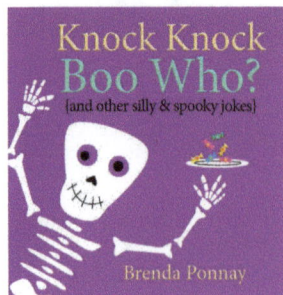

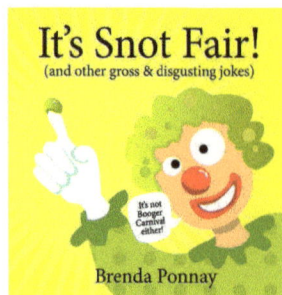

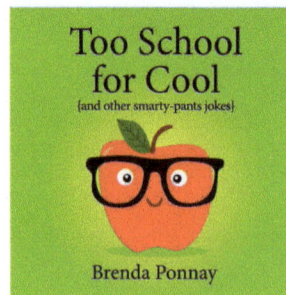

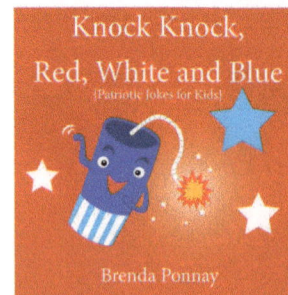

Wait, What?
Illustrated Puns, Jokes, and Weird Questions
AUDREY BEA

KNOCK KNOCK, UNICORN WHO?
ILLUSTRATED UNICORN & MERMAID JOKES
Stephanie Rodriguez
Jenna Johnston

Knock Knock, Olive You!
{Valentine Jokes for Kids}
Illustrated by Brenda Ponnay

Too School for Cool
{and other smarty-pants jokes}
Brenda Ponnay

KNOCK-KNOCK DINO-MITE!
(DINOSAUR JOKES FOR KIDS)
CHRIS ROBERTSON

Knock, Knock Monster Who?
{Illustrated Monster Jokes for Kids}
Stephanie Rodriguez & Adam Pryce

Yo Ho, Ha Ha!
Pirate Jokes for Kids
Written by Debbie Creasy
Illustrated by Sofia Zita

Knock Knock, Lettuce In!
{and other funny vegetable jokes}
Brenda Ponnay

Knock Knock Moo Who?
{and other silly animal jokes}
Brenda Ponnay

Knock Knock, Blub Blub!
{fishy underwater jokes}
Brenda Ponnay

Fart-tastic!
{and other stinky jokes}
Brenda Ponnay

Knock Knock Boo Who?
{and other silly & spooky jokes}
Brenda Ponnay

It's Snot Fair!
(and other gross & disgusting jokes)
It's not Booger Carnival either!
Brenda Ponnay

Too School for Cool
{and other smarty-pants jokes}
Brenda Ponnay

Knock Knock, Red, White and Blue
{Patriotic Jokes for Kids}
Brenda Ponnay

www.ingramcontent.com/pod-product-compliance
Lightning Source LLC
LaVergne TN
LVHW070835080426
835508LV00031B/3475